Surface Tension

Surface Tension
poems

Joe Napora

BullHead Books

Acknowledgments

Beginner's Line: "Water" in *Water* an anthology, John Roche, editor; all of "Beginner's Line" in a book by BullHead Books.
Surface Tension: "Well Perhaps," "Mail Mall Man," and "Root" in *First Intensity* #4, Lee Chapman editor; "The Bridge at the End of the World," "I Want to Die Like Victor Serge," and "On the Roar" *Nexus*, Joe Appleworth editor; "The path the way the route" as "Root" in *The Telluride Times*, Art Goodtimes editor; "This is the way" in *TIGHT*, Ann Erickson editor; "Dead Languages Again" and "There is This Thunder of Sorrow As" *OASii Broadside #32*, Stephen Ellis editor; "Blue Moon" *Poetry New York*, Tod Thilleman editor, and online at *Room Temperature*, Robert Bove editor; "The Pathology of Space" then titled "Rebuke" published as a *Buffalo Vortex* broadside, William Sylvester editor; also by *The Zelot Press*, Bill Shields editor; "A Broken Limb Upheld by the Light" *The Greenfield Review*, Joe Bruchac editor; "The Hypno-Realist Poets" *House Organ*, Ken Warren editor; The International Operator" a section in the anthology *Generations: A Centenary of American Poets*, Thomas Crowe editor: also a section in *A World Without Wars, Overthrowing Capitalism* volume six, Jack Hirschman editor; and "Catch a Falling Star and Drop It" is part three of a broadside published by Kathy Kuehn, *Salient Seedling Press*, titled "On Her Some Thing is Falling".
Porch Poems: All in a book by BullHead Books.
From the Old Country: "The Immigrants" published with graphics by Jim Lee in his *Blue Moon Press*, and as as a book by BullHead Books; "Eber", "We Argued all Night", "The Lingering Death" and "Portable Shelter" in *Portable Shelter*, a chapbook by Wolfsong Press, David Vadja editor; "We Argued all Night" also in *Uzzano*; "To a Sheep's Heart" in *Artful Dodge*, Daniel Bourne editor; "From the Old Country" in *Images* as well as in a chapbook by *sunrise / art falldown press*, Miekal And editor.

Graphics: cover photo by Barbara Schmidlapp; all other graphics by the author.

2021 © Joe Napora
ISBN: 978-1-7364198-0-9

BullHead Books 509 North Main #1 Piqua Ohio 45356

For Jack Hirschman,
    always paddling upstream

Contents

The Beginner's Line [9]

New River News
Returning the Stone to the River
Water Before / Water After
River of Sand and Stone
Oh Canada
Tequila Beach
Into the Water With Sib

Surface Tension [31]

The Bridge at the End of the World
I Want To Die Like Victor Serge
The Coupling
The path the way the route there is here
This is the way
Mail Mall Man
The Dead Line
Dead Languages Again
There is This Thunder of Sorrow As
Blue Moon Blue Moon Blue Moon Blue
The Pathology of Space
On the Roar
Pigeons
Hawk, Crows, and the Abu Ghraib Picture Album
The Frost at the End of the World
My Life is an Open Book
Bad Medicine
The Hypno-Realist Poets
Mister Whitman and Mister Thoreau Do Brooklyn
The International Operator
The Joy of My Life Taken from me
Resurrection in the Middle of the Chainsaw Meditation

Porch Poems [85]
On the Line in Fast Water
Pears & Pairs
Car Tracks Through Catalpa Flowers
The Stars We Say They Shoot
The Singer Songwriter
Rocking After Heart Surgery
The Last Wave
These Sparrow Variations
It is Coltrane's Song
A Broken Limb Upheld by the Light
Book Worm
Water Pump
The End of Poetry
The Survival of the Fitless
The Last Porch Poem
Fade

From the Old Country [115]
The Immigrants
To A Sheep's Heart Asleep in the Void
Portable Shelter
The Lingering Death of European Violins
We Argued All Night about the Beer Bottle Indians
Eber
From the Old Country

After: Water Before [127]

The Beginner's Line

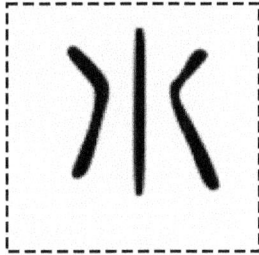

For the Boaters who got me through to the other side:

H.D. McGinnis, Dennis Garrison, Mike Graves, John Weatherford, Monica Weatherford, Randy Howell, Jeff and Brianna Beranek, Rob "Lava" Ho, Krista Gaffney, Andy and Lindsey Szofram, Lauren Weatherford and Sib Weatherford.

New River News

One

The shadow of a winter warm
as never before falls upon the land
at a time when the sun would throw
light and release water to flow.
But no. It's daffodils in bloom
and the hawks play at sex
for the promise made that life
goes on. And so it is. Spring (and all)
with no winter, weeks before the
cruelest month of Eliot's Wasteland.

The rapids of the New River are some
washed out by high water. The Dries
are low but runnable. From the train
I see the entrance to the Hawks Nest Tunnel.
The water flows over the dam
and fills the often empty stream bed. The tunnel
sucking the life of the river as it did the men
1000 maybe 2000 and the Blacks
buried in a mass grave at Martha White's
farm in Summersville. Men breathing
pure silica dust. All corpses. The corporation
Union Carbide lives on. The train rides
smooth along the rapids of the river.
It's at this point of time 80 years later
still a river of sputum, bile, and blood.
I name the rapids as the train rolls by,
rapids marked in memory of my many
misadventures. Lower Keeney, Double Z,

window shading in the hole at Upper Railroad.
From the train a passenger seeing my boat roll
and then flip end over end might think that
I was doing it all on purpose. But there is none.

We pass what looks like a large nest
in a tree at the edge of an island in the river.
The conductor announces that the train
has just hit a bald eagle. When I step down
to the ground I thank him for telling us.
He says, "I was devastated." The truth
does that sometimes. He says,
"Sometimes that helps."
My wife announces
the reported death to West Virginia birders
and soon one replies that he walked
the train tracks to discover it was a wild turkey,
Ben Franklin's choice for a national symbol:
> For my own part I wish the Bald Eagle had not
> been chosen the Representative of our Country.
> He is a Bird of bad moral Character. He does not
> get his Living honestly. ...For the Truth the Turkey
> is in Comparison a much more respectable Bird,
> and withal a true original Native of America.

A man discovers the truth by foot, and eye, and hand.
And it helps, sometimes, as the conductor said, truth will
out. And it helps sometimes. The Spanish did not
blow up the battleship The Maine. Nicaragua did not prepare
to march on Texas. The North Vietnamese did not fire
upon USS Maddox at Tonkin Bay. Iraq

had no weapons of mass destruction. Judi Bari
was not an eco-terrorist. Rachel Corie was not an enemy
of Israel. Michael Vernon Townley was
a CIA assassin. The eagle did not die.

There is more. Now an article in the *Charleston*
Gazette reports that it was an eagle killed by the train.
I read an old essay by Hunter Thompson. He says,
 He has poisoned our water forever. Nixon
 will be remembered as a classic case of a smart man
 shitting in his own nest. But he also shit in our nests,
 and that was the crime that history will burn on his memory
 like a brand."
The eagles were given names: Whitey and Streaky.
Which died? It takes two to hatch the eggs, raise the young.
Wendy Perrone who saw only one eagle at the nest said
 "It's also an accident, and accidents happen."
 I said,"What is this? It doesn't seem like a poem."

The eagle, or is it a turkey, said nothing. Is nothing.
Like Nixon, like all of them now dead or soon to be,
Kissinger, Wolfowitz, Bush (both) (and all
of their family), Cheney (and his too, except
for the gay one), Judith Miller, the apologists
at NPR, all who let it happen not once
but over and over again and over again: war
for the pleasure of killing, the thrill of conquest.

There is more to this failed poem.
There is always more. Perhaps the eggs will hatch.
Perhaps the eaglets will live. Perhaps Ben Franklin

will rise from the dead. Perhaps America will
welcome again the "tired masses" and overthrow
all of those (Olson) "who advertise us out."
Perhaps I'll get in my kayak and run
the New River Gorge backwards and blindfolded.
Perhaps it was an eagle. Or a wild turkey. A turkey
Henry David Thoreau would love. Perhaps
Henry will rise from the dead and then
give his life to stop the fracking and
the Keystone pipeline. Perhaps.
Barbara and I are taking the train back home.

And now more. The final, a parting of this way
of writing, a renunciation, a reverse Annunciation.
It is me telling on the Angel of the Lord, an angel
which in this case is this eagle called Whitey, who
is not a corpse along the railroad tracks
but is alive in flight above the river,
the New River, the oldest in America. It is
this way the Resurrection as Comedy. It is
snowing and the third day of Spring.

The train engineer told his version
of the story. I tell mine. I'm tired and so
I believe are you. The eagle rose up and hit
the window of the train engine
bounced into the air and away toward the river.
Apparently. No one caught him. He had
wings of his own and he could fly.

14

Water Before / Water After

[Fraser Champion, in Memory]

> In the beginning there was a river. The river became a road
> and the road branched out to the whole world. And because
> the road was once a river it was always hungry.
> —*The Famished Road* by Ben Okri

This ancient Chinese symbol for water suggests
everything. Water flowing downstream from a rivulet
to the ocean, the turbulence that rocks make
against water and against flesh.
A young friend and everyone loved him.

There are holes in rivers. Water is as solid
as any force of nature, a mountain of granite,
the love he had for a woman. Rosie. A rose
is just as solid. The water rushes over a rock.
The rock washes over the graveyard.

A hole is formed in the river
when the water rushes back upstream
after going around the rock. It can hold you. Fold you
into yourself. It did. A violent craving for the body,
the hunger to turn flesh into water. Everything
moves me. Moves you. And sometime
we yearn for stillness.
But stillness is a siren song for dying.
I did not understand this. The woman
holds her son's corpse and curses the Americans.

Blood is a river.
The lies of the president are a river.

His mother was at the funeral.
I said, "I loved that boy."
She said,"He would have done anything for you."

There is that Eskimo song that a friend sent to me.
Diane, how could you know?
A beautiful print with blue and white waves
in the background. All that is missing
is the color of blood
to win the national flag waving contest.
It read. It said.
But who hears the whisper of the words on paper?
Who Believes?

"Do not cry. You will come back safely."

Returning the Stone to the River

[Jesse Cline, in Memory]

To celebrate the life of their friend, fifty and more
people jumped into the cold waters below
Fayette Station Rapid, of the New River in West Virginia, expressing their
regard for Jessie's love of the river.
They gathered small stones to take with them and
return them to their favorite river as a symbolic
gesture of the ecology of sadness and celebration.

It's an unfair and unjust equation of pain
thrust upon us to balance our lives through
the dark and light as we measure ourselves
by the love we give with the loss we receive.
It is not fair. It is not just. It is what
it means to be human. Someone
well meaning but hurtful and meaning
less than we who stay silent
brings some god into the equation
and upsets the balance to rid our painful
and pity full selves of the ache that rips in to
muscle and sinew and bone
as if we should be made less, feel less
these very things that make us
that made him who we grieve
into what he was. He was a man.

We don't allow anyone to make us into children
to have him stand above us as a man. We
stand beside him. We ride with him.
He was, after all is said and sad and undone,
a river guide. We must let him take us

and balance the inevitable force of rock and wave
in the journey to some near or distant grave
a give and take, to and fro, a rock a roll
with the will that lets us go
into that true cliché
that we give ourselves up
to the river flow.

Fears and tears are what we are.
Anything less makes us less makes us unworthy.
We all are in the same boat.
We are steady and true.
We know who we must be.
We know where we must go.

River of Sand and Stone

[Jeff West, in Memory]

> Spectacular exposures of these rocks occur in the
> Grand Canyon of the Colorado River in northwestern Arizona, where they
> overlie the strongly deformed and contorted Vishnu Schist, the angularity of
> which stands in bold contrast to the almost horizontal bedding of the
> Grand Canyon Series. —Encyclopedia Britannica

Take the groover (and you must).
You shit in an old ammo can.
Clamp it down, and you carry it out
and down river with you. Left on your ass
are the grooves from sitting on the can.

That is a real name. The Stikine River.
It now has a name. Great River.
The Tlingit call it Shtax' Héen :
Cloudy River, or Bitter Waters.

Through the Grand Canyon he said,
"Don't take your schist for granite."
Not that anyone could when it's in your boat
with you. One is dark black and smooth, the
other is rough and red. But some people
only see rock and can't really get to the roll
of the water as it pushes and pulses
under the raft and kayak. In New York
at the Peace Eye bookstore it was Ed who sang,
"I've been swimming in this river of shit
more than 20 years and I'm getting tired of it."
It was the Sixties ride on the high tide
of reverie and pain. This is now.
Now it's all that is left.

Now it's all about Jeff, the Superman of the Ocoee.
Vishnu, the Hindus say, means "All-Pervading"
protector of the world and the one
who restores the moral order
of the universe. He is peaceful, merciful,
and compassionate. Yes, you were Jeff,
you who knew, who knew water as sacred.
Who knew the word sacred is the word scared.
And us as scarred. Scarred. Words
as scrambled as my feelings.
It our need now.
We want the real name for our pain
from you, to restore the moral order
of our universe. One verse and it's never
enough. Your friend mooned us as we set out
down river. We laughed. He yelled the greeting
of farewell that we could not then know
was a lie as I and there are so many and we try
to "See you on the river."

Oh Canada

{Marc Leblanc, in Memory}

I love to sail forbidden seas, and land on barbarous coasts..
—Herman Melville: *Moby-Dick; or, The Whale*

I got the call
and it was sad news
from Canada. I drove
to the lake and walked
into the wood and found
a stone shaped like the head
of a shark. The daffodils
have circled the pine with
yellow blooms. The snow
has gone to melt weeks ago
and it is two weeks from Spring.

We are all almost water.
It freezes and we break.
The snow still falls in the mountains
of Japan. We are so brittle.

The river outside my cottage in Canada
flows out of the cold north
to the ocean waters
as salty as our tears. The cry
of the loon is rare there.
Wood ducks nest in the trees
across the channel. Sometimes
the sight of eagles. Above

the rapids the flight of osprey.
For all for everyone who knew him
for a friend and brother and son
we long for time before this time.
It was then and I said
even before I had met him
to Joseph and to Jen
I want to adopt him.

Oh, the gentle and the fierce
waves of kindness he left behind.

Tequila Beach

Colorado River, Grand Canyon
You have to start some
where to measure from. A crossing.
A place. A passage. A poem.
So it's Lee's Ferry which is not
a ferry but one hundred and seventy
point seven miles from Lava Falls.

You are always, he said, always
above Lava Falls.

And one by one and two by two
we make the run through Lava
and after, after all that was said
and then done and us
undone we celebrate our salvation.

Fire Water. Old Grandad in plastic bottles.
Rum, Tecate, and PBR. It's the wild dance
upon the water. With the rafts strapped
together as if without the arm in arm
and flesh to flesh to anchor ourselves
within our mortal selves we would
rise above the waters from the water
within us which is our only holy
union lest we become the desert trail
along the river that we scouted from
brittle and hard and sharp and fragile.

We have been baptized into
shapeless shape and become
like to like unto the reach
of each of us being
as our bodies know
as water. This rapid

once called Vulcan and we
have our Vulcanalia. We are
that time and perhaps never
again joined with fire joined
with molten rock and this
is the simplest explanation

why Brianna and Jeff
and Loren and Sib and Rob and Krista
and John and Monica and Holmes
and Andy and Lindsey and Dennis
and Mike and Randy and HD and

we run and we jump back
from the desert sand
into the water.

Into the Water with Sib

Wilder. Aptly named.
My five year old grandson knows
that the greatest Greek warrior Achilles
had only one weakness: his foot
where he could be maimed.

And the stories of King Arthur's Fisher King
wounded in the leg it was he
who kept the Holy Grail safely hidden.

And Hephaestus the workers' god
carpenters, blacksmiths, builders
who made Achilles' armor and
though his leg too was wounded
he was the god of movement.

And so I was not surprised
and I was not pleased
to dream of Jesse and
the next night as it turned
to day to dream of Sib.

I had tossed and turned my way
through the night asking myself
the eternal question of writers
and of boaters: What
what is the right line?

On the Grand at The Roaring Twenties
I tried to avoid the meat

and got typewritered to the rocks
on the right. Flipped.
And rescued.

Not the perfect line. Not a nightmare
but not the best way through
the rapid to safety below.
I dreamed of it though.
I dreamed of the right way to go.

It was HD, Mike, Dennis, John. Or Ho
who showed me what, or showed me who.
I can't remember who said
"Jesse knows."
And Jesse's dead.

But he came to me.
With a slight smile and that look:
you know more than you know
if you just let your fear go.
He sat across from me.
And this is what he said—
"Don't worry. Pay attention.
Listen to your guide."

And then I woke up. Or so
I thought. And sleep walked
to the water. And Sib stood waiting.

"Sib," I said,
"I forgot something."

26

I stepped waist deep into the pool
below Fayette Station.

Sib held a brush and a bar of soap
and he said, "Look up to the rapid.
I got your back." I laughed.
And then I went under.

The water flowed over us.
And then it roared. Waves
and rooster tails.
The eddy fence was fierce
and turbulent. The bow raised
and dropped. Into the trough.
Raised and dropped again.
And so it went.

The boat rocks.
It rocks us roiled and tossed.
Tossed into our innocence.

I woke up in the shower.

"Sib?" I asked.
"What?"
"I still don't know."
"None of us do."

"But Sib. What's at the bottom of that drop?"

"That drop. Any one. Around any blind bend.
The frightful hole. We don't know.
We just go through. You go.
Like Dwayne. Like John. Like Lauren.
Like all of them. I always got your back."

I turned off the water.
Toweled off. Felt clean.

Dirt and doubt
swirling down the drain.
Gone. The V wave.
That dunking at Iron Ring.

The bubble line through Lava.
Our reveling at Tequila Beach.
The Gauley celebration after Sweet's
crowded onto Postage Due

where we closed in tight to each other
and each of us, honored to be together
as we shouted and raised a hand to our brother.

And with him in a final embrace,
it was a gift, and it was heavenly grace
from Sib Almighty, we saluted him
and saluted each other.

Some River Terms

Back Ender : The stern of the kayak goes under and raises the bow, sometimes over the boater's head.

Big Water : Large volume, fast current, and big waves.

Breaking Waves : Where the top of the wave has collapsed over itself, creating a white, frothy look.

A Drop : Water going over a ledge, a waterfall.

Eddy : The river is flowing down stream and the eddy water is flowing up.

Hole : Where water flows over a rock or other obstacle flows downstream and then back onto itself is an eruption of whitewater.

Horizon Line : As a paddler approaches a drop they usually cannot see the river below, making the drop itself look like a line across the river.

Kayak Roll : The basic self-rescue move of righting the kayak after turning over. The kayak sprayskirt keeps the water out of the boat.

Keeper : A reversal of water capable of trapping a boat.

Loops : Complete front flips.

Pillow : Water that rises up above the surface or up against a rock that sheds the water to cushion the boater from the rock.

Slot : A narrow section between two boulders or between a boulder or the bank of the river.

Tongue : The part of the face of a wave where the water seems to flow best.

Undercut : An underwater cave with restricted exit.

Whirlpools : Spirals that can suck paddlers and boats down deep under the surface.

Whitewater : Fast flowing water over obstacles in the river.

Window Shading : Rolling quickly upstream when water catches the upstream edge of the kayak.

Surface Tension

the perfect and consummate surface and bloom of all things
—Shelley, "A Defense of Poetry"

He had a tightrope walker's feel for the land beneath him—
its surface tension, the give and take of things.
—Tim O'Brien, The Things They Carried

…dissolve my soul in sleeping surfaces
—Robert Duncan, Ground Work I: Before the War

The Bridge at the End of the World

> You lift, you are the world-edge,
> Pillar for sky-arch.
> —H.D. "The Cliff Temple"

I read Tamura Ryichi's poem
called "Every Morning After Killing Thousands of Angels"
that begins: "I read a boy's poem called
'Every Morning After Killing Thousands of Angels'
I forget the poem, but the title won't leave me."
I have the boy's poem only through its absence
in Ryichi's poem and like Ryichi I think of the boy
and must also think of Ryichi and the quest in questions.
The boy's mornings and Ryichi's
how are they so different?
The boy's mornings and mine
are they different?
Ryichi's poem and mine how different?
How different are we three.
We all read the same newspaper differently.
We all read different newspapers the same.
But the boy reads a cartoon called The Wizard of Id.
Ryichi reads the financials called capital and speculation.
I read the want ads called meat and cyberspace.
The boy watches angels sliced up in cereal
like bananas of light and feathers where
the Wizard exiles him to the mean streets where
an abortionist shares an office with a nude tax accountant
and the woman lawyer from the ACLU
she moonlights at the topless bar.
Ryichi watches the angels dance
in the emptiness of the pin holes
made after stabbing in and in
to numbers that collapse lovers in

32

to dollars and to yen.
I watch everyone I love go on the auction block
or evaporate into electrons on the video screen.
The three of us join hands. In this poem.
None of us real. Which is our only point of contact.
Our hands are slippery. Blood. Sweat. Tears.
But not in that order and we do not dance.
The bridge is beginning.
The boy lays down the foundation
of a pillar made with crystal memories.
The bridge is beginning.
Ryichi supplies the plans on paper woven with alcohol
and the economics of surplus desire.
The bridge is beginning.
We all have to read the newspapers.
We are alone. Computers we never shut off.
Varieties of screen savers entertain us.
Bankers and car rental corporations are online.
On the screen a wave crashes against grass.
The shore holds up to the assault.
The grass is waved inland where lovers are lifted,
gently caressed and dropped into sand.

The boy laughs. I smile and hire laborers to bury angels.
Ryichi orders whiskey and cigarettes.
I steal dirt from the tabloids wicked rumors about politicians and
poets. I mix paper and clay into bricks and stir ashes
blow embers into fire and build the bridge from here
this poem to nowhere.

I Want To Die Like Victor Serge

It's not so difficult
to enhance an ordinary life
with drama, adventure, beauty.
All that is necessary is to risk your life
helping to overthrow the tyrants,
refuse to perform tricks for the dictators,
and be friends of the poets. Some.

As I write at a desk nearly covered
with books, a lamp with no bulb,
nine pennies, four heads up, five tails,
validating the universe of predictable uncertainty,
a postcard to send to Barbara,
a book of stamps and a folded newspaper
about uranium poisoning
from the town I lived in for 20 years,
my eyes trick me as eyes always do

the article in the paper is about another
nuclear weapons plant discovered by chance

perhaps the odds are fifty-fifty
that every town has one
that operated during the 50s
and now people, my friends, we fought together
against the dead Presidents and now the walking dead
to expose, to stop, contain, limit
the damage of their numerous wars
to preserve, protect, to accumulate
passion, pride, power and money

I read the headline "Activists request review
Group wants DOE to cover expenses"

I am thinking of Victor Serge.
We were born
in the time of the first perfected machine guns;

I misread the headline as "to cover ex-penises"
and finish the rest of the stanza
of his poem "Dialectic"
they were waiting for us, their excellent perforators
of armor plate and brains haunted by spirituality... .

You know your eyes. Don't you?
They play tricks on you.

I read armor as amor. I admire
the skill of the translator to rhyme
perfected with perforators.
I see that the word admire
contains mire and I am stuck
but I don't mind.
don't mind, no mind

Victor. Victor!
We were born in the time, my generation,
we were born in the time, my generation
of the first, we were born in the time
of the first perforated universe.
victor victor

I saw John Kennedy campaigning in my hometown
but I never saw
until the broken bodies cut and mutilated
or only bone pieces and fragments
were uncovered his plans
for the Death Squads to roam the Americas
Johnson showed us only his scars
Nixon for so many years silently bombed Laos
and that pissant Oliver North with secret plans
to put us in containment camps
even there though perhaps not
in the soccer stadium
set up by Kissinger for the supporters of Allende
there would be some beauty.

Victor.   Victory.

He died, says his son, "one day in November
of 1947." The son wasn't home
so Victor had walked on then posted a poem to him.
Later Victor Serge lay slumped down dead
in the backseat of a taxi.
The son is an artist.
He can't draw the face of his father for the police
have already covered it with a plaster death-mask.
He draws, instead, the hands.
The next day the father's poem arrives,
the last poem in this book I'm reading
this poem called "Hands".

But there is something greater than us
that has forgotten nothing.

This is the curse of the victims of torture,
the mother whose child is fragmented
from the bombs we drop on El Salvador,
Victor Jara's last words to Nixon,
my friend Lorry in Nicaragua huddled in a ditch
holding a child who pisses on her lap from fear
as Reagan's contras walk by.

I believe now.
Hands.
Not some god keeping records in the next life.
Hands working in this one.

My grandfather in the coal mines.
My grandmother on the farm.
My father repairing radios.
My mother stuffing pillowcases with feathers.

And that young man.
I never met him. The Nicaraguan boy. His hands.
I would have loved to touch his hand with mine
who held the rifle that shot down the plane
of Eugene Hasenfus the CIA pilot
feeding Reagan's killing machine.

Victor. Sometimes. Victory.

The Coupling

It seems comical and miserable that in order to manifest itself, dread, which opens and closes the sky, needs the activity of a man sitting at his table and forming letters on a piece of paper.—Maurice Blanchot

On Her Some Thing Is Falling

Name a word wrap about yourself like a sentence
stretched to protect your face from cuts and bruises
brought for you to apply like makeup to
please the purveyors of new fashion.
Name a word that wounds knowing it now has a life
of sound beyond your control beyond care
beyond longing except for the buyers
who take it and sharpen the image
drill it deep into you for a price you willingly pay.
Name a word and watch it live a life of its own
not hung about the human predicament
but free to wander aimlessly until it too becomes
an agent in some power passion play.
These are cartoon figures I write of.
They are not flesh nor skeleton only nor stick figures
mocking completion. Cut from the Sunday newspaper
any man and any woman joined at the feet
with a clip perhaps mounted on cardboard reinforced
to insure long pleasure, pleasure of a rather abstract sort,
and a hand pushing the man down on and into this approximate
woman and up again and down this man who slowly fills out
in color and in form, becomes a rounded out
character swollen and bulging at the junction of his legs, sprouting
missiles inching forward at each thrust of this hand as

it works through its boredom and its malice filling this woman
all the while that it cuts her.

She, For a Price, Accepts Her Calling
Again the images are really only cartoon figures animated
on a screen by a frustrated painter who painfully
draws each frame for a film in the solitude of a reverie he
is determined to share with us. The woman who gains
a sort of life beneath his pen is taken by two men
who handle each leg and pump them as if she is a sort
of bellows and from her fly those very same missiles charged
with a particular poison that substitutes for an enforced silence.

Catch a Falling Star and Drop It
The scene is a television, rapidly moving images. The scene
is Latin, a body's looseness, a moving that delighted and shook
a nation out of a rigidity so profound it threatened paralysis.
When she moved, we rocked. We trembled.
We finally needed to form her into a screen goddess
to control our own passion and to market these desires.
Less now, almost nothing, even the pictures in Playboy,
the pink skin against red silk sheets, even this
fails to excite anyone anymore, she is a symbol beyond Hollywood
control. She is Marilyn Monroe is Cuba. Now a certain
consistency evolves that demands its own accuracy.
It is a consistency of the Sunday comics again.
This heroic figure threatening to blow up the world
from his throne in Camelot. In the secret reaches of this castle
are the chambers of the president's prized courtesan.
The servants apply makeup and costumes and instruct her
in the art of waiting.

He enters, finally he enters beyond
the reach of cameras and politics.

No longer is anything subtle, no longer is the language
a style designed to mystify.

His words fill tiny balloons
that crowd each scene.

The starlet opens herself.

He talks and bulges and sprouts tiny fangs like missiles.

Next Sunday she will give her neck to his embrace.

Readers anticipate.

The path the way the route there is here

for Barbara

> ...One man could not understand me
> because I was saying simple things,
> it seemed to him that nothing was being said.
> I was saying: there is a mountain, there is a lake.
> —George Oppen, "Route"

It is not the eye
and no one is convinced that
sound is truth.

And smell is only memory.

It is the touch of us
somewhere

the warmth attacked by ice and cruel logic
remains like an imprint from the Cretaceous Age
two lovers, one body

I was saying: my good fortune
your beauty and such kindness.

This is the way

I think.

It is the only way
interesting
to me.

I think.

Words
such as they are

paper over everything.

No.
Under. Under. Under

just about
everything.
worth.
while.
we wait.

Mail Mall Man

for Sonny Williams

Plastic palms and pizza. Air-brush T-shirts
of Jesus and Madonna. There among the oil
and sugar the word viscoid.
Why? What does that mean?
My vocabulary is weak
my passion is strong
for coffee from oppressed countries.
It strikes at me like Wal-Mart
into the gut of the city. The silence
of the well-intentioned. Outside
teenage girls and grandfathers. Outside
smoking in bad weather.
Young boys in the grips of a security guard
at the universal shopping mall.
Too much hard dying. Too much for sale.
So much once beyond buying. And nothing,
nothing beyond the pale.
There is a rhythm to it all and it is seductive.
And reductive. Implantations. In plantations.
In the implications. We follow. The poem pulls us. In.
And in to ourselves. And in.
In to the crowd.
Rubber pizza. Veggie dogs.
Oriental chicken and curly fries.
At the International Foods Bazaar.
We look strange. And we look good.
To mirror the real each poem begins
and ends with plastic.

The Dead Line

...word-based and unable to dance...
—Keith Johnstone, IMPRO

Grateful to get the car started
grateful and surprised
hateful and wide-eyed and no not this
this rhymed hit
it is a false start approximating a lie
but grateful grateful to get the car started and surprised
and now wide-eyed to this moment we race
the engine all around all around
and around us old guys grateful and surprised we drive
we drive too fast through towns and countryside

All around us night flowers.
—Joe Bruchac, "Walking With My Son, James"

round curves where the old body swings
it swings and sways and lifts
momentarily it lifts out of the heart
the heart the head leaps into hope
we hope the car will not stall and us
stranded forever stranded far from home
and we die alone I'm trying
alone along the road
along the road a wreck
a wreck inside the 'bode the body
the body only spotted slightly pitted with rust
rust that is not cancer though it growls under the skin
and under it begins again to say
I'm finally trying until it erupts finally and finally ruptures
the body a rapture a rapture of flawed flesh

which is the only kind and is some kindness
and there I'm trying is no one to say
no one to say this is the one way
you do it so that now every time I try
try to write a poem I quickly discover I am no
no poet what a relief I am trying
I'm trying to say that I've stopped being a poet;
                          I've become something else. —Nazim Hikmet
to become something else and say
to say it is the end of the poem when
to say the poem when the blades
the helicopter blades whop whop whop
over Saigon and Nixon
took the country took the world off the gold standard
forever and forever it became
only oil and Kissinger deflated
deflated our expectations maybe let's be honest
maybe it was fire the Buddhists made of themselves
that lit up the day its gleaming
our dreaming Kissinger scheming
us poor folks us old guys the drivers of used American cars
money as fluid as blood and marrow of bone
they came on through mud offering degrees
of creative writing and the promise of publication
a long path of MFA programs endless seminars
leading to inflation and the MBA another way
to squeeze the language dry and then
like those shoes the kids kill for they pump it
up with air to stand taller with air which is not breath
but fake desire making everything   2 guys
everything but the gun making everything

all but the gun worthless worthless   2 guys

They came for him that Sunday.
— Ngũgĩ wa Thiong'o (*Petals of Blood*)

2 guys in long black coats hats gloves blue neckties
they are everywhere celebrating with Lee Iacocca
the Chairman with his ledger book red
white and blue the Statue of Liberty selling Chrysler the heart
beast of America bursting the claymore mine
and more and more and mine and mine
fragments more than any American Dream shattered
in pieces as it must to slice and to cut
for not a death honored
for not a single death reported by a single newspaper
for not a silent grieving only wondering
I walked from the newsstand to news box and back and forth
back and forth like a mechanical Diogenes and god
I want to rime the words down on your knees and god
help me not one newspaper from this land of the freebies
reported on the thirty-seven dead in Nicaragua no one
weeps here up north no one glued affixed stuck their eyes
eyes to the television screens no one
the rime screams and no one hears it
those poor people (they are us, after all they are)
for no one knows but Ollie & Co.
he do know how the blood flows
to the screen we sit before and after
and after there is nothing and after
there is silence or the roar of static
it was our mine but however yet
it was our mind
ours before and after it exploded

46

and not noticed by the poets poets who

conundra (for wch read, the insurrective)
—Stephen Ellis, "Congression: Notes" 05.04.89

want to be rock stars or cyberpunks
poets who work so hard at being so soft
in the head psycho-irrelevant like R.E.M.
saying nothing to appear to say something something is what
the fans want to say something but after all is said
and not done and they write lyrics and dress grunge new hippies
beatniks hoboes but schooled at Harvard Yale Chicago I distrust and
they're worried now they got tenure
but no audience matter how funky it is they long for a backup band a
band and a full house oh to be rock stars make millions & millions do
heroin but make it through recovery
recovery to sing the blues authentic suffering
just like the Mississippi white blacks oh oh Mississippi
singing imitation Nina Simone
is everywhere working it is everywhere
on the chain gang

I distrust the incommunicable; it is the source of all violence.
—John-Paul Sartre, "What Is Literature?"

on the chain gang the long dead line Rock & Roll
as Muzak on the elevator music going nowhere
but up in the supermarket with Whitman
and the rhythm of money
The Stones on Lawrence Welk music
while Bobby Hampton dying and the singing
Let Him Bleed and nothing solid but the things
of my days are hard language
refusing to soften up with anyone's blood out in my garden
while Lee Iaccocca sells Liberty and the talk covers the crying

47

out in my garden it is not blood
Robert McNamara is not climbing down and down from a tree
down from out on a limb escaping escaping the dogs of war
but they are not dogs they are ghosts
and he is irrelevant to them and he
and he is not relevant to me
irrelevant to this black walnut dropping nuts into the garden
dropping and some sprout and a dozen or more I mow around
and around them and they grow
and I set to work and it is not work
each spring morning it is pleasure
but I set to work each morning before and before
and before the dryness of summer stops the invasion
I go out into the day at the beginning of the dimming night
it is all transition the killing that I do
it is transition and a translation thinking of politicians
so many so many millions dead and I blame them
no forgiveness no forgetting not here where the words are
there is no blood I find the snails

> The poet speaks the poem as it is....
> —Wallace Stevens, "An Ordinary Evening in New Haven"

I find the snails still shelled and the slugs
and salt them and down they go
they go slowly shrinking down
and leaving a slime trail a trail that as the sun
as the sun lifts the heavy shadows how they linger
and it lights us all for there is nothing else but it and us
the light is now heavy there and these trails where the slugs
the slugs have shriveled into nothing but light reflections

Dead Languages Again

for Ryûichi Tamura

The notes   These notes obscured by my hand
blurred   writing blurred from too much good
whiskey   too Is there too much   even ever
                  I keep hearing him say it ever even
now here   while his liver shrinks and shrivels
                  fluid into knots for love lost
here now   even as his hand shakes as he writes

                  nowhere in the fawning eulogies
                  for Reagan NiXon I can't
that word   find the word fawn it's not the deer
not that dear   not Thoreau's deer not Bambi not mine
deer reader   where we lay naked on the blanket
                  and we washed the sand away in the waves
goodbye   it's the blood   sometimes I know that
and oil   those NPR with their smirky giggles
and coal   when talk gets serious

here   when not one of the said Here
it is   Here lies here lies here lies
                  the son-of-a-bitch who killed Neruda
                  Here lies the son-of-a-bitch who lies
lies   here there here there lies the son
                  that sets on us all
lies   and Allende and Victor Jara

                  and here lies the son-of-a-bitch the Sun
sets   setting once and for on the West
                  And then

And then   more of my scrawl left on the end pages
of Ryûichi's book to remind me to write

this poem   this poem but it isn't this one but that one
in that one was a line of giant XXXXXs
        the giant X of niXon

X   it's by design for EXXON get your X on
They win the prize for the double X
Stolen from Dos Equis beer

Ken   you bastards but no one
Saro-Wiwa   and no one

asks the otters about EXXON, the fish

Xed out   and the birds oil bathed X'd out

Into a particularly ugly kind of breakage
Neruda and Allende and the mangled

The Body   body of Victor Jara they cut off his hands

Like some scene from Spartacus

Crucified   hung up to dry on the wooden X
NERUDA ALLENDE JARA

X   them and us the crime the time the rime
Kiss

When Kissinger dies will the ghosts walk by
like in the old John Wayne war movies

$30 billion his friend Secretary Al I'mInCharge Haig
and Bill Moyers praising the mysticism
        of hate mail

Shell's oil loot Clintons & Kissinger playing Strangelove

Who   John Mitchell playing the warden and the con
                 The hundred thousand suicides of Viet vets
                 And the million upon millions
Who   voted for Nixon and Reagan twice
Who   one X then XX marks the spots   millions
                 Upon millions of cancers upon the body
        politic in the heartland of
                 Lee Iacocca's Chrysler America
Believed
in satire
and then   twice: rice & lice those are the rimes
They killed him people not voting for hope but voting fear
for being   not mass culture but mass idiocy
                 and fruitloops and new anchors
                 with short skirts and big tits
subject of the
Laughter   and fields of blackberries
Of the people   nine Nigerian environmentalists with their bodies
on the line   on the line hung out on the line
For the people   and fields full of blackberries
By the people   the line of the oil company's ledger sheet

Leo Frank   Ken Saro Wiwa swinging to the tune
Jewlynching   the Shell game the name game: We
KKK-BBQ   a responsible corporation
                 The word sheet sheet sheet echoes man
she-e-et
                 The white sheet sheet man
The berries   Cecil B. DeMille and the Ten Commandments
     on   Charlton Heston and the NRA on the
  mountain

the bush   with Moses lobbing & lobbying bombs
burning   on to the Palestinians
           And Billie Holiday singing strange fruit

           I bent down and the blood stain was still
           upon the soil the blood not mine
           But only one in a million could see it
           Let it alone feel it
He wrote
Strange Fruit   the berry on the bush
And
was mistaken
           the weight of the black birds

(Abel Meeropol)
           In the field with the Mollie McGuires hung
for a black
man   By Sean Connery on the
    late-night movie
           In the field with the Haymarket Martyrs
           Martyrs to what? The 8-hour workday
No one   no one cares because they don't
   measures
           their work by hours down time
Shell: 30   because they don't measure anything
Billion   except by dollars and the stain

           And the stain was upon me
           And it formed the pattern of the alphabet
I am   upon my fingers and everything
A man   everything like a mush Midas I touched

```
                        Turned upon my spit
                              For it was my mouth
                        That made the word stone
                        And the words died on the page
A man of peace  rigid and occasionally golden
Of ideas                but they are not for sale  except
                        For what was in the field was also she
                        The Lady Billie Holiday singing
                        And Victor Jara singing and even
                        Old Joe Hill & Phil Ochs singing
                        And Joan Baez singing about Phil Ochs
                        To the tune of "Joe Hill"
I dreamed               "I dreamed I saw him last night as alive
                        As alive as you and me"

Appalled
At the
Denigrating                         and 3 thousand mothers

Poverty                             and 3 thousands lovers
Of my people                mothers and daughters and fathers
                        Lovers my brothers singing

                        Young men hanging
                        On 3 thousand mint julep tree
                        In the heart of the south
                        These mouths still singing
```

There is This Thunder of Sorrow As

The snow flakes the sky breaks the demon eyes
the miss takes her lemon thighs to school
the crow shakes the reason why
how else to fool you into believing the sound
the ground moves to the noise for the boys at the chemical plant
Ashland Oil refinery of all of your sensibilities advertising We
Support Education
with a gentle mix of gases explode the words above our house
windows shatter the progress of the snowball
before it gets to hell. We feel safe.

it is only thunder the newspaper headlines scream
no one heard the explosion and it was only thunder.
No one heard the sound of one body falling
into the Landwehr Canal.
No one heard the engines roar of the cars
of "the BMW Brigade." The Frei Korps who joined up
with Hitler's storm troopers now read *Soldier of Fortune*
and collect checks from Washington and play.
And they play. And they play.
Little torture games for the rich boys to play.
And play in El Salvador. Roses. Is Roses. Is Roses.
Luxemburg's body thrown into the Love Canal.
Her last essay titled "Order Reigns in Berlin" order that
"inexorably proceeds toward its historical fate—
annihilation." The bumper stickers
while I was at the grocery stuck on my car:

We 🖤 Ashland Oil.

Blue Moon Blue Moon Blue Moon Blue

for Alison & Jason (June 29, 1996)

he has forgotten nearly everything everything
he once thought necessary necessary to remember
and remember and remember remember what is it
that needs this thought to remember not this
not any this not what is at hand in the hand
a bird is worth more one bird one hand
clapping in celebration one hand reaching meeting
one hand reaching out and meeting all hands
all hands clapping all hands on deck
and there is no captain speaking there is no captain
all hands on this deck here here&now
and there is no remembering with everyone here
this deck this gathering this celebration
all hands clasping

a union and here it is where the meaning of union begins
every time and I don't need to remember for it happens
every time the word union is an onion
sliced and sliced and to cut into it many times it is water
the water comes out from within and it flows
and the water flows out and carries us with it and we flow
together in this union and there are tears and no sadness
in this this is the beginning

a union has begun long ago but it is here
here where we are now here nowhere
nowhere other than here the beginning of politics
the beginning of friendship the beginning of family
they said it long ago and they say it now
they say it here&now

one big union and I hear it one big onion
we peel it back and there is no center that we are not of
there is no boss that we are not of
there is no onion or no union that we are not of

there is a moon that is the onion that is the union
how the pull of bodies like to like
moves the tides of change of constant change
which is a pattern as predictable and as wild
as this union we are here for we are here for this
or we are here for nothing at all
and so the moon takes us as fully as we can take it
as full of life twice blessed
the blue of the sky is the blue of the sea
and there is nothing to separate them
for they are one together with the other
and there is this place
this place where we are gathered in gardened in grown in
where all paths lead and try to trace them out
no matter how wild wild and tangled
and seeming to go everywhere and nowhere
now here again and again
and if there was a captain on deck
he would shuffle us and shuffle us
and we would be thinking
and saying to each other as we shuffle along
some path we would say we would say
look at me shuffling along some path this is fun or not
and even if we think we know or knew the combination
of any cards that we were dealt that have our face
in the place of king or queen or knave

and we are all the jokers there is no reason to mention
that we make up a pattern
a hand that is us and these directions
these directions lead here we are
the hand that is played now
we are here together and there is no single winner

we are all the winners no one before the other
no one leads no one follows the leader
all and all to win all to the winds
all taken shaken all mistaken
all together now alle alle in free alle alle come in free
all together now in this union

no memory no remembering nothing but being here
all together no captain no conductor no leader
of the chorus of course on course or off course
just this union being here now here
all together now everyone now all together all in free
all together now in this union

The Pathology of Space

Start
with the wreck
start with the wreck
the car the carrier

but call it
call it recognition

the subject is knowing
and
know again
that the vehicle
the vehicle was never new
the vehicle is history.

To think again is the way
it's the way we think at all.

I see now
I see why we gringos forget. Why
the lowly immigrant sheds her rags
why she chooses designer jeans
jeans riding up in the crotch

so uncomfortably. Why the past
becomes an embarrassment. Why ...

why it is only a question
a question of survival. Only.
58

Only these lonely.

They line up to pledge before
the television; it is better
better to live half-formed,
better to live with holes
in the memory,
better to never know the history
of what is possible.

(Shays Rebellion, Nat Turner ...)

Better to have never heard the cries
of the Haymarket martyrs, from Spies
from Parsons, Ling's last lament before
before he places the dynamite cap in his mouth, or
did the police really kill him? Even better

even better ...

better not to know the joy
of the victory at Homestead.
We might want more, we might risk everything
to feel so good, the way

the way those steel workers did
fighting and winning against all odds
against Carnegie and his hired thugs
against the Pinkertons
against state power.

The state power, our own power turned
against us. Think, when, when,
name one single time did the state help us?
Now name one hundred where the state troops
fire upon the innocent.

Who can face the terror of the accumulation
of promises lying broken about the memory
of what America could have been?

My uncles never wished to hear the story
of the Molly McGuires. The shadow
of the gallows silenced them. They
were not cowards, they fought down
each day the fear of the depths of the mines.

My own grandparents, they could
only see streets paved with gold
when they looked through the glasses
tinted with Seagrams. The coal dust
washed down with fire. They watched their hands
strangle their own throats. Knowing

not to be a Hand is still the struggle,
or a Head, or any single body part.
Cock. Ass. Tits. To be

a Body. Who knows what that would mean?
American is a legacy of dreams
of what that would mean. That it would be.

60

The real American Dream. What is that?
There is no image of wholeness to guide us.
Not Horatio Alger. Not Lee Iacocca. Not Bill Gates.
It is such an image that kills us.
Capitalism is not that dream. We crush
our brothers and sisters using them
as the ladder of success.
Stairway to heaven.
Jacob's ladder.
We watch the blood trickle down.
Not that.

There is a lack.
A hole. And that is what we guide by.
Even the holes in our memory,
even these are signs
pointing to recovery.

Any other drive to wholeness is a suicide.
The car skidding over canyon walls.
Our own exhaust, the tube in our mouths.
If there is a way, it is the way
of indirection. Easy
too damn easy to get lost.

I would like an image, I would
like to fix it long enough in my sights
to destroy it before it is used
used to destroy us. My friends

so many of my friends give themselves

to nature. No doubt
the mother confronts us all. The rhythms
of the blood are the rhythms
of the sea. Salt. Sweat. Pulse.
Blood flows at the call of the moon.
And yet. And yet …

No natural law is natural to us.
Natural law is a prescription
for same damn concentrated poison.
Is a restriction
for some people wrapped round
with wire electric and so pointed.

If there is an image
the image is a Nazi caressing a flower.
The U.S. Supreme Court sentencing
homosexuals to 20 years
in jail for sodomy. Or Maximiliano Hernandez
who wouldn't step on an ant nor eat flesh
killing 30,000 Salvadorans.
Farabundo Marti murdered.

Or that arch nature lover
Ronald Reagan. What Christian
doesn't believe that
to see one redwood is to see them all?
Everything is mapped and measured. Nature
disappeared with the urge for money.
Nature finally blotted out
with artificial light.

All concentration is killing.
All capital is concentration.
Yes, a camp for our fear of the future.

There is no wilderness
to hide in. Each spot is an entry
in some banker's ledger book. The attack

must be, the poet's attack
is on every possible front
and every front is possible. Every form
is suspect. Plato
is mental play dough
forming, foaming at our mouths.
The Platonic monsters are everywhere
and we oppose them with the only weapon,
the weapon ourselves a multitude,
the plural minorities—Indians, Blacks,
Palestinians, peasant, monkey.
We Shall Be All.

For the primitive mind there is no art.
All is art. We are not no-nothings.
We have no privileged moments.
The proletariat will not save us.

But consistency will ensnare us.
We need to be on guard not avant-garde.
We need provocations not vacations.
We need to be guerrillas against the gorillas.

Every limit becomes reasons to die
for god, flag, family. We
need to learn the hardest thing of all,
the reasons to live.

Art captures ourselves in an embrace of success.
The poet must stay outside of everything
but herself. Any invitation by the king
is a warrant for her arrest. Kennedy or Bush
or Lenin or Stalin mime Plato's Republic.
Better to be banished than be the banquet.

Poets need not defend their many selves.
The scientist needs to beg forgiveness for Hiroshima.
The politician for Dresden.
The chaplains, teachers, congressmen for Vietnam,
killing witches and Cambodians.

Ronald Reagan scares us
because he is only an image
of what we allow ourselves to become.
He is nothing, nothing
but the new Will to Power. A void.
Emptiness.

Only an empty nest to hatch our fear
full wishes for the normalcy of death.
He is the image
of double-talk, of Wilson, Truman, JFK.
He is the killer rabbit of our nightmares.
He is Ronald McDonald the American clown story.

64

The Avenging Angel of plenty
striking down the disabled.
"Suffer the Children to come unto me"
has a new meaning with this new war, not
on poverty but on the poor.
Reagan is the ultimate image
for he is nothing, the negative capability
of our inability. He
embraces all: the Four Horsemen
handing out candybars, codeine, cokes, cocaine.

I think of the Wobblies.
They taught us how
to be slippery, to keep moving, to keep
from making an easy target. They
taught us how they lost
when they stopped laughing, got

respectable they took themselves too seriously
to jail. We need to look

look at how we make our future.
We accumulate the images
of horror as we surrender to the horror
of images. We fall prey
to slogans of our own making.
None-the-less we pray:

To sustain our past
as it sustains us
until we redeem our country

from those who accumulate misery upon us
by the destruction of our brothers and sisters
from those who try to convince us that
there is not struggle, that
there is not a continuing, a continual moving,
a process, that there is only
that final space
a resting place
who try to convince us that
time will be conquered
who cannot see that space is only time,
a bit slower, a time
to love within.
Protect us from those who try to
convince us that
there is not a future, that

there is only
the end.

On the Roar

Starting at the tollbooth with the money in my hand
staring at the dictionary handing words over to the man
it's all currency it's all flow it's all going going go

> [Latin fata, factum, fate: goddess of destiny,
> fari: to speak, Fr. feé, Italian fata,
> "fay" and "fair" derived from Middle English feyen,
> AS fegan, to agree, fit, join, bind, also "fee" payment]

It is agreed we have a mutual need
and I'm on the road

with my son reading Kerouac and me reading the road
back unless this way we hit the road running
and spinning in a metal mash
fire and slick and pain it's the tune
we don't want to play too soon

but sometimes sometimes sometimes you get played
you get tuned tuned to weird music
music not like an engine
an engine humming through these mountains
Rte 64 with Joni Mitchell hot again for a new generation
as hot as my brakes as hot as my temper
as steel turned to a knife edging away from bone
to cut like the pain of America this

paved paradise and built a parking lot
for all these rich kids
heading back to Vanderbilt & VMI Subarus and Volvos

the occasional Neon that I pass with little effort
in my old Chevy Caprice it's a Classic with 240,000 miles
between the hands of some worker
and mine holding tight to the wheel while the singing goes on
the beat does the club raises
and the rain falls and the wipers move me

but only occasionally do they shut off until the engine is done
and only occasionally does the engine shut off but keep dieseling on
like it knows more than I know like it knows
that if it stops it won't start again like it knows me

and the engine isn't shutting off until we pass
through the tunnels from Wytheville Virginia through Bluefields
through these red whiteandblue fields

where they driveby shooting off their images
honest to god Americans who are old enough
to have voted for Nixon twice driving
their Oldsmobiles and Buicks
and young enough to have voted for Reagan twice driving
their Cutlasses and Thunderbirds and I pass them
me old enough to have not ever voted for a winner
except Clinton but he doesn't count
because he is no winner and I
I'm as unreal as they are
passing through unreal mountains as unreal as the unreal city

because if I don't shut off I'll shove them
over the mountain railings
and into the valleys awash with water streams flowing

the rage of water and the rage of a slightly crazed and tired
over fifty poet who is happy his son isn't some little
yuppie bastard who thinks Newt Gingrich and Bill Clinton
and Oliver North are men

a son who likes music that brings memories up from the deeps
where the illusions are long and hairy and wrapped round
with tie-dyed fantasies of revolution that myth
that sustains us like Hermes
that slightly over fifty poet
I want to pickup Hermes who waves when I fly by
How did he get on the road
He never left it, Jack
but I can't stop and neither can he go
until the spirit moves us both
until the winged words move you
Hermes perennial hitch hiker
and the waters keep flowing and my car going
and that's all that matters
the words lie about the road
littered language we pass by
for the rich kids can't make it through these mountains
any faster than I can in their cars that cost more
than I paid for my house and they can't drive
only push their expensive machines harder on the road

but I catch them up on the curves even if the chevy sways
it's okay
it's eight cylinders against four
lexus or solar plexus
and I'll win every time

because for all their money they have no skill
they have overkill like B-52 bombers and nukes
and napalm and agent orange and smart bombs
and I have the rage and they have stupidity and money
and rage wins because I won't forgive them
for their supplying the contras to kill the hope of justice
for their being conned by the politicians
for their forgetting that there was once an idea
an idea that illuminated the world
and the idea was justice
(not just us not just us not just us)
the idea was freedom
(not flat tax freedom not homeless freedom
not Gulf War Syndrome freedom)
the idea was equality
(not OJ Simpson equality
not Madonna equality)

and the idea is to get around the curve and over the next hill
before the transmission shifts itself silly into oblivion
the idea is my car
my car the working class 240,000 miles of work
born in the usa miles of work
my car dies and we all die
the junk yard of history
some kid with a squirrel rifle shooting out the headlights
some kid with enough sense not to vote for politicians
who screw him
some kid who won't fight a war while the rich boys watch
some kid who will take his rifle and find better targets
than animals

bankers and lawyers and chief executive officers
and politicians who want
    some kid to love napalm and
    some kid to beat up drunks
    some kid to love anthrax and phosphene
    some kid to follow orders
    some kid to love to rape Japanese children in Okinawa,
    to rape Cassandra
    some kid to love to torture Dianna Ortiz in Guatemala
    some kid to say Yes Sir I'm only following orders
    some kid to throw stones at anti-war protestors
    some kid to bomb Iraq to assault Troy to burn witches
    some kid to kill flag burners abortion doctors
    homosexuals gypsies jews Emmett Till
    some kid to join the CIA FBI NSA ROTC ARMY
    some kid to hate poets who want
    some kid to love
    some kid
    walking through the brush looking for squirrels
    looking for hickories
    looking for a home in this earth
    that is not a graveyard
for me or for my old chevy
struggling to get over the mountain to get home
where there is some peace left to keep
in this time over the mountains
and through the snow
earth mother grandma old car son jack on the road
let's go

Pigeons

The people of London, having developed a technique of living
in the face of repeated danger, now accept the preposterous,
and what was until so recently the incredible,
as the normal background of existence.
—H. V. Morton's *London*, February, 1941

And so it is with Americans.
The thieves come out to play
and the people open their purses and pockets.
It's no different with language.

I robbed the Indian storehouse
of words becoming an accomplice
to New Age shaman showmen. I just reached
out for something, an act of resistance.

An act of helplessness. Just an actor
in a bad play on words. It wasn't my fault. It was
mommy's daddy's default programming.
The chief called out to the bear
"Come on down. Come one down.
We need to kill you." And now.

Old Bob Barker mouthing
The Price is Always Right
come on down come on down
since everything has a price. The last war was a joke
that kept recurring
as I switched the radio dials and each station
had the same message:

The old man said to the young woman,
"Would you fuck me for a million dollars?"
The woman whispered, reluctantly, "Yes."
He said, "How about for five bucks?"
        She said, "What do you think I am?"
        And he, "We already know what you are.
        We are just haggling about the price."

So I blame the priests, the old marketers
new tv showguns, all those
pious X-ians making the payoffs. The righteous
playoffs against the muslims. Everything

for sale. They moved the cemetery, dug
up the bodies to make room for the Wal-Mart. The woman
accepted the folded flag from the coffin. The Iraqi
people wanted to be free. She sold her boy's
body for a slogan and an assfuck from
the president. Pound's old bitch gone dead in the mouth

no barbarians at the gate, already inside, laughing and dying
to get that signing bonus and a college education.
Within days of the broadcast of the planes
slamming into the two towers, poor people in West Virginia were
sending money to
the families of the victims helping
to make them millionaires, a transfer of wealth
rivaling the best scheme that Ronald Reagan had imagined.

[No one sent a dime from NY to the families
of dead miners. No one.]

73

I managed. The only thing left to manage. To
remember. To not forget. The only left. The most
radical. The old woman on the park bench feeding pigeons.
No dental plan. Black holes for teeth. Mumbling her history
to the birds. How she organized the wives of the strikers
to shoot back at the hired goons. Blair Mountain. Matewan.
How her old man died broken and bitter. I stepped
on the pieces of bread, grinding them into the sidewalk,
shooing the birds away.

Her face twisted in anger.
I walked on happy again.

Hawk, Crows, and the Abu Ghraib Picture Album

1.   The poetry readers have been tortured
enough. Enough he screamed. But this is not news
for the readers of difficult poems. They must think
they are still alive. Those hard cases, poems
that repeat words words that give the illusion
of rhythm, eye candy he called the pretty and brain
less blonde even though her hair showed black
roots he wanted his lies and lines
to break along the hidden fault lines
to make the clever ones his club his friends dig
into the language rubble for hidden treasures
that they could steal and sell to the degree museum. There
are no pictures of tortured hooded spread armed poets.
They walk free through the home of the brave protected
by machine pistols and smart bombs and
their utter invisibility.

2.   The KAW KAW KAW is a world of sound
that only the hawk takes seriously. He fears only you and me
the inconsequential as well as the sequential line
of black words on the page. The red
tail, red shoulder, the falcon, the carnivore, the cleanser
of the slow, weak, witless. There is no symbolism here
of Blackhawk Down. This is the world of extreme deception
of lives wasted away from false promises fake prosperity
only alive within the covers of some book. The crows
are calling outside the window gathered in the wild
cherry tree the ash and the walnut wailing the warning
while the hawk sits with nothing but hunger holding
it to the perch above us all. His silence is all knowing.

His language is the word made flesh
as it is ripped and torn from the bookmen
unaware of the wounding they bought and brought
down upon their own separate selves.

3.   Mr. Nobody paddles his kayak over the waterfall
and as he reaches his paddle to the lip
of stone to propel him forward into flight he says
I am a man without ambition. Some, but who
are they?, would say without talent without knowing
without rhythm and timing without without and
I agree with that with myself being nothing
at the stillness at the mouth of the drop

The Frost at the End of the World

It's only those who glimpse the awful, endless corridor
of death, too gross to contemplate, that need to lose themselves
in love or art. —Jim Crace, "Being Dead"

Swollen waters of mulberry, apple, and peach frozen
rubbed crumbled dried flakes of the promise of late summer harvest I
blame every early death on Bush and Cheney.
I release the waters welling up inside me
little rivulet signatures of misery through the dirt
on my face my nose dripping into my mustache.
I piss on an imagined president. I expect my ears to fill
with blood & I want to cough up phlegm and fluid of hate
& despair & I sweat through the frost as my mouth dries
to dust. I'm the desert. The sun has gone down in the west.

The clouds have lifted and the moon shadows the fox
in my yard. Weapons of fire and water. Torture the news.
Berry blossoms browned.
No cherries to be plucked
like new recruits on the streets
of Baghdad. Anticipation of the juices.
The late blooming apples or peaches
above 3000 feet. Flowering
with the promise of the marine recruiter
handing out money and college degrees
and a blank check for a future formed
in a desert latrine and the sound
of the laughter of old men
drinking single malt scotch whisky.

My Life is an Open Book

Libro, cuando te cierro
arbro la vida

Book, when I close you
I open life
Pablo Neruda, "Ode to a Book"

It's only phantom pain. The VA hospital is filling up.
Each family's bank account is emptying out. I sit
in my backyard and know that the Redtail hawks are dying.

It's all about frogs and appetite
and concentrated poisons and language
that is as toxic as Round Up.

I empty cardboard boxes full of words.
I gather myself together at the strip mall
built up on an old strip mine.
I talk to the security guard about stripped minds.
He tells me about a girl named Katrina
raped and waterboarded with a can of Pepsi
because a black girl in West Virginia
ain't shit. Now ain't it the truth.

I say that's nice. You got your facts
wrong. And I wouldn't call it
poetry. The USA is a giant
company town and all
of your fancy words are nothing
but worthless scrip. The Chinese
have pulled the string
wrapped 'round your nest egg.

There ain't no middle in middle class.
He says Move your car
or we'll tow it away.

Two deer race across the driveway.
A Coopers Hawk feasts on a Blue Jay.
Okay. I turn the page. Turn down
Peterson's Guide and stare into nothing.

The feeders are as empty as a blank page.
I can hardly read anything at my age.
Everything has to eat
something. "I don't understand

a human being doing another human
being the way they did my daughter,"
Carmen Williams told The Associated Press
on Tuesday from her daughter's hospital room.
"I didn't know there were people like that out here."

Bad Medicine

We're a bunch of cab drivers trying to deliver a baby.
—Stephen King, *Duma Key*,

I sit in the roost, a room I built
attached to my garage where I watch
the birds and the squirrels stealing
the birds' food. I sip good bourbon
and read bad novels. And I've learned to love

Stephen King. You think
George Bush is bad, but
King is Bad in the good sense. And
you have to empty yourself
of the pain. His crimes will never
be answered for. He and Cheney
will never be put up against the wall.
You won't get no satisfaction Mick.
Stephen King knows more than
you do, much more than I.
So if you've gotten this far through
these poems, and there are parts of your mind
that say, yeah, that's right, that's the way
it is. You're wrong. There is no way.
A man walks down a road not
noticing the burnt out land because
he is burnt in and out. He talks and shouts
but only speaks to himself. He prays
for rain and only gets ash and dust
and newsmen giving homage to
each other. That man knows more
even than Stephen King.

The Hypno-Realist Poets

All of my poet friends think I've lost
my touch. My other friends don't
know whether or not I had one.
What? The Midas touch? The itch
to scratch a mosquito bite or
poison ivy? We all lose it, what
ever we had or didn't. It's a hat
protecting your head from the bite
of the sharp end of a broken branch.
We need that. What? That hat. Every time
I hear a poet read on NPR, I cringe. I'm embarrassed
for everyone. If only I could count the syllables
of the poem and determine the length and width
of the world of lies and half-truths
that the poets and politicians utter with
such sincerity. If only I knew the math
I'd offer friends and foes
to sit with me and share a glass. There
is enough in the bottle and just
enough chairs for us all.

Mister Whitman and Mister Thoreau Do Brooklyn

This one who wanted to be every man
and that one who wanted only to be
a man walked along the river bank.

And everything presents itself
to perception as perfection. Lilacs

in a vase on the table where an old man
sits alone wandering his mind
towards his final breath.

On the long legged desk sits
a finely made pencil dividing
the last notes of a diary from pages
never to be marked and marred.

A cab rocks through holes filled
with water. Mosquito larvae spill
out onto the dirt. Conversations

end as abruptly as a coronary
or as protracted as a lingering cough.
Somewhere along the river the child

with a fishing pole finds
a white cloth stained blood red

in a puzzling and improbable pattern.

The International Operator

He has an ancient crank telephone
bought at an auction. He turns the handle
and generates enough current
to make his genitals stir and swing.
He connects to the long distance operator
where at the futbol field, Santiago Chile
the nameless ones are being executed. Victor Jara sings
sings his songs that attempt to make this
poem whole. Somewhere

midst the fragments of pestilence
and pain the black and metal rain
drops from the telephone wires
and forms the name
Michael Vernon Townley
who assassinated Orlando Letelier
and then the names Nixon, Kissinger, and Bush.

In Spanish the guards they listen to
his last words, See-ya. And the cord
is coiled about the neck of the nearly naked
teenager as she reads the love poems of Neruda.

The man from the CIA listens.
He tries he attempts to keep his body from moving
from turning turning into dust. Her words
shuttering and shattering against his ear. She
gyrates her young and nervous hips and hangs
herself upside down over the living room couch.

The company man turns
the language of love in
to the language of the killing field.

The image in the poem deep into
the scars scares. The concentrated
power. Greed. Lust. Distance. Longing.
The burns the wire makes on the genitals.

Sitting on a wire a black bird's claws
wrapped in a circle close in
to a noise squeezing cutting off into
a gasp the last song of a man condemned
to never know that as he falls down
he lifts us. He is that kind of man.
We are that kind of fool.
We dream of a hand on the trigger
ready to harvest bankers and politicians.
It's late. I cannot sleep.
Even in a fever my grandson

who is barely one reaches
his arm lifting and I
hold him up for his hand to play
along the light switch. In the morning
in the distance it is light enough to see
the gathering of mercenaries. The cold reality
of things wraps spirit round sound
and the words he learns are not names of objects
but activities made real by resistance
to his fingers. I whisper words

84

he will one day understand.

And the many meanings of words
all words do not disturb
him or me. He will know who
is the enemy. He will know what to do. This
is the time for singing and a time
for grieving. It's better
better than all of this bleeding.

The joy of my life

taken from me
a red tail hawk in a tree
sixty seventy feet
a wild cherry and me
in the still point
of a distant presence
in a surround of crows
caw caw cawing the measure
of their annoyance and now

my displeasure hopping
in a flutter of feathers
to another limb and sound
broken as I am
with the turmoil of crows
diving at the hawk crying
denying their impotent
attacks at the hawk's
assured complacency

he is no red tail
he is impenetrable
he is the product of myth
he is the American eagle
he is an armed drone
he is madness and mayhem

the attack continues
the crows scream

the ultimate predator sits
denying its fate
to have turned into metaphor
sad symbol of power and pain
the wastage of liberty and life

there in this distant view
the birds me and you
there's no eagle no crows no
walnut and cherry tree

it's smart bombs
Fallujah Baghdad Kabul
abstract and distant killing
a remote electric claw
and the caw and call to this

the crows scream
remember revolt resist

Resurrection in the Middle
of the Chainsaw Meditation

for Barbara Mor

It was the first and only one not
a model for anything but a sign
of a better time when

democracy is not for sale. When
the world of men is at peace
with the earth. But no. I witnessed

a sacred act as holy as water
carrying my kayak over rock
and the roll to the surface

from the perpetual baptism
of taking water as one's savior.
The wind took two wild cherry trees

and kissed them to the ground.
I cut a hundred feet of thick and true
logs for my son to use

someday. Boards, beams, perhaps
a sanded smooth cherry post or two
in his heaven of a house I'll not

live in. The last cut slipped ten feet
of timber to ground and then
the remaining tree lifted

and planted itself into the hole
it had made when it fell. I thought
it will live again. Now

without limbs to weight it down
it will fly and fly and
take me with it. I'll not cut

the last ten feet of timber.
I will not. But
if you have read this far

through this poem you
know that this majesty of a tree
will fall again.

Porch Poems

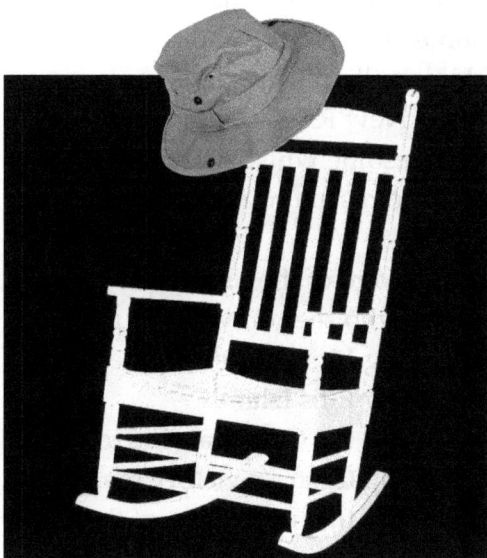

The Line in Fast Water

{4-17-1991}

Happy happpy happpppy as if
As if As if As if As if that is
that is the New Year's game
no pain they say no gain

AS IF. Of course one thinks of Mallarmé
the mystery
                    flung down
                                screamed
and
        at the edge of the void
which is nothing more and nothing
less than the whiteness
of the paper and Snow
arrives. I mean the doctor
for that was his name. And
home birth was his fame.
Hank Williams dies after the cross
of the New River. The train blows
its lonesome whistle. The raft guide
looks to rescue someone. Something.

At the edge of the uncertain
a man who sees only his daughter
following Lincoln freeing the slaves
following Ellis Island
following the Canadian Citizenship Act of 1947
following Castro's victory march into Havana
following the indictment of the Watergate thugs

following the enactment so many years later
of Civil Unions in New Hampshire

There is such a thing, a vague and never to be
defined thing, such as hope. As a future bright

bright light
                    a site
        into the New Year's
Canadian night

Pears & Pairs

{4-17-1961}

Sitting in the newly painted porch
watching a squirrel play among
the branches of my pear trees
and two red grosbeak peck away
at the near ripe pears and the sun

the sun it warms my face.
The birds, the squirrels
opening the skin for the bees.
I'll not get many pears this year
from these two trees
planted twenty years ago
as my Meridel Le Sueur Memorial.

And now it's a grackle feasting by itself.
She served me pear sauce once
in St. Paul. These trees they never
live alone. And the pair of them
in Bisbee that one summer.
Meridel and Barbara Mor.

 To let the sun heat her legs. The warmth
of the desert moon would come
later. The two women not in this
anthology that sits next to my coffee cup
now shaded as I write: *Generations
A Centenary of American Poets.*

That was no grackle. It was
a long tailed brown Mocking Bird.

Not black at all. But a black winged
butterfly sits on an opened rotting
pear harassed by a wasp.

Soon the trees will be a swarm with bees.
Barbara and Meridel. And Sharon Doubiago.
So many poets giving over their lives
to beauty, that fierce and thankless
struggle. I should have culled the trees.

On one branch ten ripening pears
that will not get full size. Yet
as the bees attest they are sweet
but out of reach. And yet again
I celebrate this abundance.

Car Tracks Through Catalpa Flowers

{6-21-2015}

It's the Solstice and we stop.
As if snow on the road is possible

on the first day of summer. Blanket
is the word. Everyone

uses it for snow and you
can use it now

for this road turned white
on this summer's day.

You can't avoid it.
You can't go around.

You pass your way through.
And crushed flowers are a sign

of your passing. Your tracks.
It's you. Drive the car.

In a short time, too short,
the flowers fade into brown and gone.

KAW: At Home in This Wilderness

{5-21-2015}

In the land of fragile hopes
and faded dreams begins
a fire to light the memory
of distant and present atrocities.

A murder of crows it is called
of these dark birds gathering
in the upmost leaves and limbs
of the Beech saved

from men whose mission
is to turn maple and oak, ash
poplar and cedar into timber.

And so it is. That crow as I remember
Is at home. And if, then so am I.

The Stars We Say They Shoot

{5-21-2015}

One.
After a night of meteors' flight first
in a line east and then to west
as if flung a flaming spear from
a distant sun announcing here I am
a sufficient god for everyone.
I wonder where are the mosquitoes.
Why does that farmer's mule
and why the cows express
their all night discontent?
Another falling rock across
the Great Bear's seven stars
and the flame of utter and final
transformation. Against
the haze of a distant village light
the bats sweep overhead. I thought
I must be going blind in the morning
when to celebrate I read "The Comedian
as the Letter C". He would laugh in opposition

Two.
Stevens offers two august propositions
that "man is the intelligence of his soil"
and "his soil is man's intelligence"
and I see not his distinction not
one better but both. And Crispin?
Where after all is sad and done
is as he says of him a clown
"but an aspiring one." Is this
enough? Enough to get Charles

into the poem? Isn't it not so much
about Gloucester? But any place?
Such as the Georgia man
"walking among pines
Should be pine spoken."
My Charles is a crisp one.
Up right and up tight
not to learn what Williams did
and Stevens it is in his words:
"The plum survives its poem."

Three.
And so the stars turn to earth.
No angels my friend Jack Clarke
(I do like writing that)
yet we only met
but once with Ken in Buffalo.

I think you had misplaced
a particular concreteness. It is
this that remains: distant
memories and those projectiles
in the sky above, and this protracted
and protective verse: Ken, Jack, this
a book of collected poems
on the porch of a house half
built in Tennessee. The dolphins
breathe oil and leap no more. And so
the stars they return to earth.

The Singer Songwriter

{9-11-1973}
It is also necessary to explain why,
under certain circumstances, a "simple" "folk" song
may have more human value than a "complex" symphony.
—John Blacking, *How Musical is Man?*

I would like to believe
that we call Autumn Fall
because here it is in middle September
and the slight breeze provokes the high and low leaves
the ash, maple, and the beech and that young sycamore
leaves which dry as it is clunk to the ground
and the tulip poplar turns green to brown the leaves
they fall to the earth which is the home of all.

It is spring time in Santiago where people gather
to hear the poet Victor Jara play
but Richard, it is his call, Tricky Dick kneels
and Henry Kissinger smiles

and this Fall is a state of mine and yours
but I doubt the name is just
and true but as the hawk
its shadow sweeps across
the grass and trees
I have to ask you
but cannot. You

Rocking after Heart Surgery

{5-10-1919}

Five days after my son's birthday,
and I don't forget Karl Marx
but wrote the card that sits still
yet moves me with hope and tears.

Dew on the orchard grass and
the shine of spiders' webs.
The plum and pear, cherry and
paw paw that strange fruit.
It's all newly planted and
it's all as old as yesterday's news.

The sailors raced through Charleston
with clubs and knives. All dark
skinned peoples seek the night.
Over the hills and through
the dawn breaks. Us?
We sit at rest. The hand
made table of three-inch thick
slabs of white oak waiting
for the mist to lift
out of the valley.

The Last Wave

{5-5-1983}
For Jesse Cline,
Fraser Champion,
Jeff West,
Marc Leblanc,
Sib Weatherford

A hand raised. V.
It will happen again. See.

The current.
Your boat.

A wave.
I shout out
at you. I
miss you.

These Sparrow Variations

{5-21-1969}

The Nest

A blur of red a sight
a smear of light

red cloth of the boy not blood
of the young one caught
swimming shorts
a blur of a red stain
a blur my eye held in for a moment
a blur for a moment

a red blur
the red shorts the color of

then I lost it
then I lost attention
focus clarity lines and shadow

until I saw his probing stick
until his probing stick opens
his probing stick opens and opens
opens the nest and

his probing stick opens the nest and midst
the falling grass and straw

I saw the dried grass fall
the falling grass and straw
three barely feathered sparrows
to the ground fall

three barely feathered sparrows fall
to the ground and the boy
to the ground and the boy leaps
leaps off the picnic table and he starts
with stick in hand

after each of the sparrows gathered
one then two gathered
two in his towel and I
with some affection
frantically searching
searching under the overhanging limbs

under the limbs of a fir tree
the tree offered a sort of shelter

oh the stupid stupid sparrows
sparrows too
too damn simple to build out
out of reach
with a simple trust
to build out of the reach
the thrust of this boy's need

The Woman

A pin of light
reflected from her glasses
I see I hear
she said those people they
choose their fate
arms open to the sun
to the gun
to bombs they are a falling
and words that matter as much as flesh matters
as much as the cry of the sparrow
and a song that crowds in
crowds in upon itself and repeats and
it seems to vie for attention

listening to the medley of voices that wake me
wake me every morning
every spring and summer morning

so that I rise before the family
listen to the constant song
singing of birds I cannot identify

to write about the constant slaughter
of the people I cannot identify
of the killers who I can
for it is the slaughter
we are all bloody from

as if these barely feathered sparrows
welcome in the pointed stick
and big guns from Washington

to write about the singing and
to write about the slaying
is to accept the immediate
the sound pressing upon the senses

the land is distant the land is mine
as my backyard songs combine
unto a noise the noise wakes me from a sleep
my own voice changes
changes all the others
as all the others changing me

The House

San Francisco at the dead end
of the cul de sac. A Sixties child.

The sparrows first claimed the house
then later it was the grackles marching
marching around the ledge and around
and circling the birdhouse I built
this house to attract the useful birds
the mosquito eating martins

they march and then they appear again
and again they enter each and every
hole of the house and in their methodical

investigation the images in me awakened
images of Roman legions
and the National Guard

each probe into the hole forces me
each probe each penetration opens my eyes
to a vision of Ronald Reagan
of El Salvador
of the colonels we held in power
of the dying of the archbishop

I project carnage onto the birds' curiosity
it is of course not them I blame
rape and murder in the backyard
in the yard and above my garden the feathers
the grackles the iridescent black feathers catch
the sun seductive shine beak claw and blood

It is Coltrane's Song, A Love Supreme

{5-27-1951}

The Redtails glide and silent
five Cardinals sit this Spring
in the budding pear trees
that I call Meridel's Grove
and un-silent the hawks trumpet
their frustration with
an Annunciation
of sex and savagery.

The constant call rings
us round and round
but the smaller and the swifter
hear and ignore and wait
for the seed and grain
my bird lady will bring again
and again. Again.

A Broken Limb Upheld by the Light

{5-27-1647}

I rocked back and forth as the sun broke
out in an opening of clouds.
A cloud crack. A rift. A pain.
Two weeks of overcast skies and drizzle
mixed with hard rains. Damp
into bones. Mildew. Mist.
There it is.
There it is.
Love on the line
in this delicate
balancing, a piece—
can we possibly reconstruct
how it happened?

A piece of this tree
—a walnut, black—
had fallen. It landed not
on the earth but was so
precariously balanced
on a light pole's glass lamp.
Nothing shattered. You. Me. The wind

the wind makes a quivering,
it runs through us.
It moves us. Within. And out.

We may balance in darkness,
we may balance on the light.
We may. Or might.

Yes all that happens.
And more. And more.

More he said. The witch
the witch is burning.
And yet. There
precisely and specifically so
even as it must be
as the broken limb does fall.

Book Worm

{7-23-1967}

The cold sweat
on the hot streets.
She asked if I wanted to
join her in the shower.
Instead I finished the book
I was reading whose title
I no longer remember

Water Pump

{1-24-2015}

Going down and under
a crawl space with nails
threatening an unprotected head
I wonder about Pinochet and friends
in Portland where the new nazis
thrive. And here where my friend
the poet Barbara Mor dies. There
is no eternal return. I wish her pagan rituals
would conquer space. But I have no time.

Under the cottage porch that John and Tim
and Erek and I built one week of beer, water,
and sun, and those materials that joined us
the saw and hammer, the wood, nail gun.
In spite of Ted Bundy being fried & died
justice is always denied.

The carpenter bees chew
near perfect circles in posts and beams
and when I pull the pump
under the house to hook it
to the pipe, the pipe that connects
us to the water gathered in
a hand dug well, it is then

it is then that one solitary carpenter
bee proceeds to sting me.

Of all places it was on my ear
and I suppose it was from its need
not necessarily to hurt but something
something like a lesson
something like a revelation.

A bee not known to harm anyone
is telling me to buy a gun.
For the first time
my life is governed by a rime.

And then when I crawl out
from under let them come
those Trump supporters
white nationalists corporate
crooks and cops. I'll have it all
and ready all of the time.
A thirty aught six, a lightweight Colt
and one more, a Glock one nine.

The End of Poetry

{11-14-1996}

And the End of Time
I should have included that
in the poem's title. No one
or maybe two or maybe one
but this is the language
we are stuck with. No one
reads it. And for certain
no one heads it. And who
should after all listen
to any poet?

There are leeches in the slack water
of the river that flows this river
that I see from the cottage porch
which as I said I built with my son
and friends. And John, John Kelley,
let me name him for he is gone
but not forgotten not as long we
who loved him so remain, John, Csaba
the only one from those days when
the simplest of acts was to oppose
the Vietnam war. Csaba Polony exiled
from the invasion of Hungary in 56.
Mac, Maurice McCrackin who married
me with Barbara, and that other
Barbara Mor, who like Ken Warren,
my literary companion of forty years and more.

Who now is left (and who is right)?

114

Not Karl Young, for he too died
and it was, let me say it clearly
and more clear than any prose,
he died from Republican policies.

Thomas Crowe, Bob Buckeye
from those Deertrack Days
with Ted Enslin, and now
an ocean away Chris Barron
who I will never meet, she
would have loved being with us
when Ken, Bob, Roy Skodnick, and I
visited Meridel in New York City.

Meridel, she refused to be photographed
in front of the Rockefeller Center, but accepted
graciously the Dell Comics Wonder Woman Award
and spit & shit (metaphors) on
Henry Kissinger. I've never been
so gracious and so kind.
It is not the time.
Time heals no wounds.
Like I have said before
in a violent but more gentle time
time heals no wounds
the wound is time.

The Survival of the Fitless

{11-29-2019}

It is with some pleasure this view
through the looking glass
window out to the edge
of the logged over woodlot.
Some. There she is oblivious
To me or any other hunter.

The back porch collapsed
and the woodrack crashed.
A Zen moment I wished
I could have avoided.
And would have had if only
I had added
blocks and braces before the cord
of split ash firewood
the best though not
the heaviest but
it was green as green
as I was green
before the years passed
since I first learned
the gentle art of the chainsaw.

That deer that was once
our resident from the wild
living under that other porch
facing the orchard of pear
and plum and cherry and peach
that deer that one just out of reach

of any kindness except
self-reliance if there is such
and perhaps but not much. So
life goes on but now we know
we are totally fucked.

The Last Porch Poem

{4-17-1944}

The house sparrow still nests.
The robin will always seek the worm.
The forsythia fence roots at will.
The vines eventually smother the pine.
The kudzu in the back lot I dug, cut, scraped
into piles, let it dry, let it burn, like water
it too will always win.

Potted plants, three hot peppers
that I've cut for three hot years.
The mother-in-law's tongue
also called viper's bowstring hemp, lovely,
and for the first time in 20 years it flowered.
Two avocados dug from the compost
cactus from a plant I bought 28 years ago
1991 that memorable year
but who remembers?
A second cup of coffee.

At six in the morning it is one or the other
write the poem or play the card game
minus ten for the Jack of Diamonds
and nothing until Hearts are broken.

Fade

{4-8-2020}

My love not fade away.
    {Buddy Holly, The Grateful Dead)

The forsythia flowers have faded
into a dull yellow but the dogwood remains
bright against the darkening sky.

My new neighbor walks with Grace
a Pug who meanders like an old drunk
on its tiny hurried legs.

Bill walks sometimes with Grace
the quarter mile to the Dollar Store
for groceries, medicine and more.

I don't know his last name but we talk
like old friends and his wife peeks
out of isolation, smiles, and nods.

Our front porch is as wide as the house
and welcoming. For now only the masked
mailman comes. For now he smiles and nods.

From The Old Country

The Immigrants

It is how the light is fixed,
how silver salt preserves that time
from fading. The image surfaces.

A man in what must have been
a borrowed starched shirt and a coat
tightly restricts his frame sits
his hands surround the boy
who will be my own father
who also exists as memory.

His brother sits and two older sisters stand before
a backdrop of a fake prosperity.

This constant paradox, the mundane miracle
the mundane miracle of photography
of a sudden surprises me. This
public memory, this abstraction
of the body alive in its fullness
clipped, cut, captured into
a vision pulling me to its vanishing point.
Who is it that are ghosts
when this immigrant family only has value
in an art that has so little value?

Of course. This is also who I am.
But these photographs cannot speak.
And there is not the tradition
in our family for stories. Yet
from some need my mother speaks

of my father's dead sister
Stella, lighting this void
in our personal history.

This photograph reminds me of Icarus,
Brueghel, and Williams' poem. This
man's hands distinguish the pose
from countless others. And in life
he was only his hands and
their largeness and strangely
delicate features must not have been
remarked upon in the mines. I ask
about Stella, whether she was beautiful.

As a child she looks out with an intensity,
from Middle Europe the face of a star
so fashionable once. Recurring again.

The Williams poem is often used
as an example of pure description.
Not just a non-symbolic poem
but an anti-symbolic one. A fall
is only a fall. A man
a man working
is only a workingman.
The picture it shows the sun falling
into the water and it too has remained
unnoticed by the critics and poet
as unnoticed as Icarus by the plowman.

It is possible that both the sun
and falling man took the same time to set.
That is a fool's bet.

A sun setting is more than a sun
and a man working more
than a workingman.

Stella? Stella. I knew your son, and
disliked him. He was raised by my father's
step-mother. Spoiled, everyone agreed.
But not Stella. She discovered that
she discovered that she was pregnant again
by a husband she tried to separate from.

And she made her difficult way to the water.
Climbed the chain-link fence. I imagine
she cut herself holes in her clothes
on the barbed wire guarding the city reservoir.
And she forced herself
and she faded under the water.

To a Sheep's Heart Asleep in the Void

for Tadeusz Różewicz

Everyone must sometimes rest,
the principle of fairness demands it. Even love
must sometimes stop out of self
inflicted duty. This beast believes in you
only when you stop believing in it.
And then only for a moment.

What irony.
What a pitiful finale.
You give up believing
only in your self.
Long years of darkness
have acquainted you with tragedy.
To rest means death
for the beast and for yourself.

Would it be a surprise,
a denouement, to know that you were cheated?
It was something else,
even I,
that killed the beast.
My knife.
I present you to the light.

Portable Shelter

A new pioneer
the old man calls him
pulls inward. Tempered, beaten,
ground from an old file
his draw-knife shaves
curls of bark. Long lines and rough
form a pile at his feet.
The wood must be made smooth
as a song long on vowels
swept by the wind. With
care for the blade
the knots are rived.
He has chosen trees crowded
and young stopped
with a one-inch top
and six-inch butt.
Claimed from the worm.
18 poles tied mark the center.
Pine, spruce, heavy hacmatac,
and one cedar for the lift
pole. All shaved smooth
and sanded. Oiled, caressed,
pointed to bite the earth.
An anchor offering no resistance to the rain.
Not lost is a pain
that grows from hope denied.

A worm's slow progress
inside. Eating
a path that has a beauty

of its own. A poem
written in cursive.

Minute attention given to each letter's
cutting edge. With due respect
to this poet there is
his gross neglect
of the materials. There grows
no lodgepole pine. The damp
proclaims itself. Moss
grows on cedar shingles.
A sure sign if only the mind
humbles itself to the eye.

Two hundred yards of canvas
and two miles of thread
are the signature of the days
and nights of work that measure
this shelter. A tipi
designed for the Plains.
Mildew on the north.
Fiber rot.

Yet not all is lost to decay.
For six months he shared this
second skin. Wife and children.
The moon's several faces.
And the softened shadows of the sun.

The Lingering Death of European Violins

In the shadows before dawn I watched my father
exact his ritual. From an old canvas he pulled
his father's father's ancient violin. I sat
with a shovel across my leg and was quiet.

In the ground he placed the bow and then the violin,
and I was left to fill the hole as best I could.
Dirt hitting the strings made sounds I don't want
to recall. He was in the house by then, leaving
these sounds for me, and for me alone.

The next few weeks he spent carving from cherry and ash
a new banjo. When he needed a cover for the drum
I brought him the skin of a cat that had frightened
the birds from a feeder he built when he was young.

He played constantly upon that new banjo, painfully
learning new rhythms and old mountain tunes.
Finally he was able to wean his fingers from the bow
that he had always used, and could pick and strum
as well as anyone. When he died, the instrument

was mine by right. The strings hold a fine tune
except the fifth. It strikes the note I heard
that morning, reminding me of a ritual performed
only once, for me and for the man teaching me
to let go of a beautiful and a deadly thing.

We Argued All Night about the Beer-Bottle Indians of Jasper, Wyoming

These paper walls of the motel break
down to the splintered bottle
breathing moonlight.

With love gone it happens this way,
a necessary trap of emotion. Each time
you tell me of my blindness I see

your nipples move to hardness.   You
explain the myths of Coyote and Raven.
How the Trickster allows the ravaged to dance.

"In the morning they'll be back
for the refund on the bottles not
broken.   Why break them?"

To hear the music of the night.   The way
their dreams become solid
when they shatter.

Eber Hopper

He was coming at noon to show me where
to sink a well. I read everything I could
about water tables, rainfall, and soil
structure. I didn't want to be totally
ignorant of the process. But when he
came there was no time to talk about the
pros and cons of divining rods. No time
to discuss spiritualism. Not even time
to get up a membership in a new cult. He
just reached for his forked stick. And
found water.

From the Old Country

Old woman unwinding her heavy knot
of hair.   Mane of a horse,
or the tail thrust
like the banner of a Cossack
into the wind of her youth racing
racing through and through
the sensuous dance of wheat

like the black ship piercing waves
that carried her from the old country
to her black-faced husband
who found work in the mines.

Enigma of my youth.
She speaks a language I never learned.
How can I share the secrets of this
unravelling of hair she never cut?

The faded, red velvet curtain
opens on the last act of a melodrama.
The bent, grey haired old woman
becomes the captive princess of my fairy tales .
        Rapunzel, Rapunzel
wind swirling through the golden grains
waves into whirlpools of a ship's wake
knot of wood raised in relief
on the grey weathered barn siding

        Let down your hair.

After: Water Before

My old high school's name was the best I could imagine: Mad River High. It was changed to Stebbins High, substituting a bureaucrat's name for a real one. That may have been my first awareness of the importance of naming. My trip through rivers and poetry has been my way of looking for the connection between names, what we call things, our self, and the experience of what it is that is named, real names for real life.

In the Grand Canyon, on the Colorado River above the Lava Falls rapid there isn't a perspective to guide by. As you approach, the obstacles aren't visible. The current is deceptive. It moves, seemingly very slowly. It pulses, a great up swelling of power that gently lifts the boat in a rhythm that feels like you are pulsed with the river's heartbeat. The river is in total control. The massive ledge and the hole behind it in the center, that's the place to avoid. But how? Instead of looking down river, Rob Ho in the kayak next to mine tells me look down into the water. Look at the bubble line, tiny bubbles that rise from the deep. They do their dance along the kayak guiding the way. The line is to the right of the rock ledge but not too far right where the shoreline rocks await; to see the line is to not look for it. It's to follow the bubbles as they skirt the ledge and lead into the chaos of the V Wave: Charybdis and Scylla reenacted with a frightful Ulysses in his kayak on a freezing cold river under a punishing desert sun.

Hitting the wave and being pushed under from water pounding from both sides into the deep and then up and out, I know I've been blessed with good fortune to be upright in my kayak, though turned around somehow and facing upstream. I smile and think of the poem I hoped I would write. But there was more to paddle to get to the refuge of Tequila Beach, and I stroked into the current moving to the middle and the waves and holes that once terrified me, thinking that I had learned something about paddling, about writing, about myself.

The ancient Chinese associated water with the moon, the feminine, with flow, with fear. Like no other element, we connect with water. We are water. 70% percent of the earth is covered by water, 70% of human body is water. Perhaps that is it, water inside and out, essential to life, essential to living life. And always there, always here: fear, fear to learn from, overcome, move beyond.

I've been a reader of poetry most of my life. A writer at thirty. A whitewater boater only since age fifty. I have few regrets, but not having started kayaking earlier is one of them. I think I would have been a better writer. Writing and fear? What's the point, what's the connection?

Any genuine writing is a trip into the unfamiliar, unknown territory. And the biggest danger for the writer is a success that makes that trip comfortable, the writer complacent, satisfied, even longing for the familiar. The most famous twentieth century poem in English is *The Waste Land* by T. S. Eliot. In that poem and others he had written about water. In his "The Dry Salvages" is a memorable quote: "I do not know much about gods; but I think that the river / Is a strong brown god—sullen, untamed and intractable." And another whose truth cannot be denied: "The river is within us, the sea is all about us."

In spite of the magnificence of his poetry, there is something that rings false about these lines, untrue because unearned. Except when stepping into a bath Eliot never got his feet wet. And yet. He understood the intimacy of the connection of water with fear. This

134

line from "The Dry Salvages", less true for him, applies to my whitewater companions: "Not fare well, / But fare forward, voyagers."

Inspiration Point. At a bend in the Ottawa River overlooking a rapid called Pushbutton, a play spot at low water, is a stone bench and carved rock face that commemorates boaters who have loved the river and the river community. Marc Leblanc's name is carved there. When I wrote the poem upon hearing of his death, it was an inspiration. And it may not be a poem at all. But it is my favorite of all the poems I have written. It flowed as water does. Word for word, wave upon wave, no thought, only the act of words seemingly acting on their own. Whether a poem or not, the writing tripped me up, it was a trip into the unknown, and it connected me with Marc who had kayaked solo down through the Grand and happened to flip in the Roaring Twenties rapids as I had.

A run down the Grand or the Ottawa or the New River or the Gauley is my way of seeing what's true. And testing what's true in the writing. My whitewater friends. They never set out to teach me anything except to follow the right line. On our Grand Canyon trip, at the last of the Roaring Twenties Rapids, I followed their rafts in my kayak. They ran straight through the crashing waves. Instead, out of fear I wavered by trying to turn into the calmer waters of the eddy to the left. I hit the reactionary waves and got typewritered across to the right side and flipped against the right side wall of rock. My friends, friends who I had just met days before, rescued me as I knew they would. Boating. Writing. We fuck up alone but we succeed together.

Water After

Years later at a talk about poetry in Buffalo, New York, I spoke of the bubble line in relation to poetry. I didn't say anything about fear. But there is a fear in writing poetry, a fear of looking foolish, fear of ridicule, a fear of attempting a different line, one that makes someone uncomfortable, makes oneself uncomfortable.

I remember less about that talk than I do about the rapid, Lava Falls, but I was trying to invoke an analogy that does what good metaphor can do: carry a reader across from a shared known experience to another lesser known, or known but only through hints and suggestions, or even feelings probing the complete and sometimes frightful unknown. Perhaps only whitewater paddlers would understand how putting faith into this shifting line of tiny bubbles as a guide is a reasonable and safe thing to do. When Rob pointed it out to me, I had my doubts. In this regard, whitewater is like poetry when we make our way through the line of passage from confusion to a necessary certainty, not to a guarantee but to a resolve, that the way is real, is really there, and it makes sense to surrender to the process, the river, the language, moving, the flow, our boat, the universal, mythic, carrying us forward and beyond.

Colophon

In ancient Chinese, the oldest image of the word for Water would be a mystery to most people, even contemporary Chinese. But it would be instantly read by any experienced boater.
It is a map of the river creating eddies as it flows between rocks. But it is more than that. The more you know of the river, the more this word reveals: the eddies are formed by rock to reverse the flow upstream.

This back and forth dynamic inheres in the word as it does in the real. At least it once did. The phonetic alphabet of necessity abandoned the Image. It was a gain for the spread of literacy but also a loss. Turned on its head, the letter A evokes a bull's head, the plowed field, transport, the world of work, a constellation.

Some of these poems were written in the late 70s, some in 2020. I've also made them into books and combining them have tried to make this one into a book, a real book. As Jack Spicer said of his poem-books: "Poems should create resonances. They cannot live alone any more than we can."

Unlike those individual books with their varied fonts, this one uses only two: Palatino Linotype for the poem and essay texts and Gil Sans Light for front matter and quotes that, I hope, throw light upon the poems. Published in the year 2021, perhaps to be known as the year that Donald Trump inadvertently revealed the roots of American style fascism and, thanks to Stacey Abrams and the Black Lives Matters movement, revealed how to revive the near moribund US Democracy.

BullHead
Books

www.ingramcontent.com/pod-product-compliance
Lightning Source LLC
Chambersburg PA
CBHW071945100426
42736CB00042B/2007